SANTA FE WIT

Things To Do, Places To Go, And Kid Friendly Restaurants

by

Jim Arnold

All Rights Reserved

Legal Disclaimer

About the Author

Jim Arnold is a grandfather, businessman, author and attorney who lives part time in Santa Fe, New Mexico. He graduated Cum Laude from Georgetown University with a degree in economics and received a Juris Doctor degree from the University Of Virginia School Of Law.

INTRODUCTION

Most tourists are familiar with Santa Fe and know that it is one of the most desirable and beautiful cities to visit in the United States. Santa Fe continually ranks each year in the list of top ten cities and in October 2013 it was ranked No. 2 in the *Conde Nast Traveler's* annual Readers' Choice Awards for all U.S. cities. *Travel & Leisure* in November 2012 voted Santa Fe the second favorite city in the United States, just behind New Orleans.

As the second oldest city in the country, and located in the Southern Rocky Mountains at an elevation of 7,000 feet, the city has an average temperature range of 44 to 18 degrees in January; 65 to 32 degrees in April; 83 to 53 degrees in August (with no bugs and no humidity); and 67 to 36 degrees in October. There are over 300 sunny days a year in Santa Fe (New Mexico is the fourth sunniest state in the country after Arizona, California and Nevada).

With a population of 68,000, Santa Fe gets an average of a million visitors a year. It is known as the "City Different" because of its rich history of Anglo, Hispanic and Native American cultures.

The city has almost 300 art galleries and is the second largest art market in the United States, second only to New York City.

According to *TripAdvisor*, Santa Fe has 429 restaurants with every kind of food imaginable. In April 2013, *Livebility* ranked Santa Fe as one of the Top 10 Foodie Cities in the country.

Similarly, *Sherman's Travels* in June 2013 ranked Santa Fe as having one of the top 10 farmer's markets in the U.S. And, also in 2013, Santa Fe was named on *Wine Enthusiast Magazine's* Top Winter Wine Wonderlands emphasizing Santa Fe's outstanding culinary scene. In May 2013 *Travel & Leisure* ranked Santa Fe as one of the best beer cities. In July 2012, Santa Fe was even judged the Best Food Town in the country during the *Rand McNally/USA Today* Best of the Road competition.

As for outdoor activities, on October 8, 2013 *USAToday* picked Santa Fe as one of the top mountain biking towns in the country. And, *Men's Fitness* ranked Santa Fe as one of the top 8 cities in the U.S. for trail running. *U.S. News and World Report* listed Ski Santa Fe as one of the best things to do in the city. Others have reported "some of the best skiing in the West" (*Examiner.com*); and numerous hiking trails for all levels that are "plentiful and diverse" (*USDA*).

Many other awards have been given to Santa Fe in the past couple of years. *USA Today* on December 6, 2013 voted Santa Fe the best U.S. city for shopping with New York City, Chicago, Nashville, and Las Vegas ranked second through fifth. Other awards in 2013 included *Kiplinger* which rated Santa Fe as the fourth best place to live in the country; *Conde Nast* voted Santa Fe the second best place to visit in the country; *Destination Weddings and Honeymoons* picked Santa Fe as one of the best places to have a wedding; *Travel and Leisure* picked Santa Fe as one of the best girlfriend getaways in the nation; *AARP* included Santa Fe as one of the sunniest places to retire and number four of the healthiest cities to live and retire in; and, *Liveability.com* chose Santa Fe as one of the ten most romantic destinations in the U.S.

All of these accolades primarily relate to Santa Fe being a great city to visit for couples and singles. But what about the kids and grandkids? *Today's Parent* did list Santa Fe as one of the best family destinations.

As you will find out, Santa Fe is also a great place to visit with children. The rest of this book will give a season by season description of 40 of the best indoor and outdoor things to do and places to go with kids and grandkids along with the 20 best kid friendly restaurants in Santa Fe.

Note

Hours and ticket prices, where applicable, are subject to change. Please call in advance to see if there have been any changes.

TABLE OF CONTENTS

Chapter 1

FUN THINGS TO DO ALL YEAR ROUND

INDOOR ACTIVITIES

Santa Fe Children's Museum

Where did Natalie Portman take her 2 year old son and Neil Patrick Harris take his two year old twins in 2013 while they were in Santa Fe filming movies? The Santa Fe Children's Museum!

This is the number 1 children's destination in Santa Fe. It is a great indoor and outdoor museum with interactive hands on exhibits too numerous to mention. Kids love blowing bubbles from the indoor bubble making pool and the use of other water toys as well as the trains and arts and crafts. Many enjoyable hours can be spent in this must see museum.

Located at 1050 Old Pecos Trail, one mile south of the Plaza. 505-989-8359

Winter Hours September through May, Wed., Friday & Saturday (10am-5pm), Thursday 10am-7pm (**all kids free** 4pm-7pm on Thursdays), Sunday noon-5pm. Closed Monday and Tuesday.

Summer June-August, Monday noon-5pm **all kids are free**, Tuesday-Saturday 10am-6pm, Sunday noon-5pm.

Admission fees-NM resident $6, all others $9, children under one are free.

Santa Fe Climbing Center

Northern New Mexico's only indoor climbing gym featuring a bouldering room and a top rope/lead climbing room with a large selection of routes for all levels of climbers. They say that if you can climb a ladder you can climb their walls. For ages 5 and up.

Hours: Monday & Friday 3pm-9pm; Tuesday & Thursday 9am-9pm; Wednesday 3pm-10pm; Saturday noon-8pm; Sunday 10am-6pm.

Rates:

Day Pass $14

Student Day Pass $12

Child Day Pass (under 11) $10

Shoe Rental $3.50

Harness Rental $3.50

Call about discounts 505-986-8944

825 Early Street, #A

Harrell House of Natural Oddities and Bug Museum

See a collection of 2,400 spectacular mounted insects, arachnids and other arthropods from around the world. This museum also has dozens of arthropods including tarantulas, scorpions, millipedes, centipedes and other insects.

Hours: Monday-Friday 10am-6pm, Saturday 10am-6pm, Sunday noon-5pm.

Fees: Adult $5, kids 12 and under $3

177B Paseo de Peralta (in the DeVargas Mall) 505-695-8569

Genoveva Chavez Community Center

Kiddie pools with slides; 50 meter indoor pool; full size gym for basketball, volleyball, and racquet ball; fitness center; ice skating rink with rentals.

Hours: Call for the hours of different activities but basically open from 5:30am to 9:45 pm. Public ice skating is from 9:45am-6pm.

Rates: Child 1-10 $1.50, youth 11-17 $3, adult 18-59 $6, and senior 60 plus $3.

3221 Rodeo Road 505-955-4000

Rockin' Rollers Event Arena Roller Skating Rink

This roller rink offers public skating sessions ("family night" on Fridays). The rink also has lessons and rentals. Snack bar and music.

2915 Aqua Fria Street 505-473-7755

Santa Fe Farmers' Market

Ranked as one of the top ten farmers markets in the U.S., with 100% of the vegetables, fruits and nursery plants grown in Northern New Mexico. Music is provided and special events are held often. In the Winter, the market is indoors in the Farmers' Market Pavilion.

Sundays there is a Railyard Artisan Market in the Pavilion featuring live music and over 40 artists, including fiber art, paintings, hand blown glass, herbal products, sculpture, photography, jewelry and much more.

1607 Paseo de Peralta (at S. Guadalupe Street)

Santa Fe Farmers' Market, Saturdays: 8am-1pm, Tuesdays: 3pm-6pm. Free.

Railyard Artisan Market, Sundays: 10am-4pm. Free.

Fort Marcy Recreation Complex

This recreation complex and area features an indoor heated 25 yard pool and tots pool kept at a temperatures of 83-84 degrees. The complex also has a gym. Kids 0-10 cost $1; 11-17 costs $2; adult 18-59 $4; and seniors 60 and over are $2. Monday-Friday 6am-8pm, Saturday 9am-4pm; Sunday closed.

490 Bishop's Lodge Road 505-955-2500

Santa Fe Southern Railway

Ride 1920s rail cars along a 129 year-old rail spur from Santa Fe to Lamy. Ride the train along an original route in the high desert. There are day trips, night trips, holiday and special event train rides. Snacks and cash bar are available.

The Southern Railway is temporarily closed but is scheduled to reopen in March 2014.

430 West Manhattan Avenue. 505-989-8600

Museum Hill

There are actually four museums on Museum Hill, which is only a few minutes from the Santa Fe Plaza: the Museum of Spanish Colonial Art, the Wheelwright Museum, the Museum of International Folk Art, and the Museum of Indian Arts & Culture. Children particularly enjoy the Museum of Indian Arts & Culture and the Museum of International Folk Art.

Museum of International Folk Art

This museum is home to the world's largest collection of folk art in the world with over 135,000 artifacts. Children especially like the Girard Wing which features toys, folk art, miniatures and textiles from more than 100 nations.

Open 10am-5pm Tuesday through Sunday, closed Mondays. Free 5pm-8pm Fridays Memorial Day through Labor Day. Closed New Year's Day, Easter Sunday, Thanksgiving and Christmas. Adult admission is $6 for NM residents, $9 for nonresidents; youth 16 and under are free; students with id get a $1 discount.

710 Camino Lejo

Museum of Indian Arts & Culture

This museum tells the many stories of the peoples of the Southwest through art and objects such as pottery, baskets, tools, jewelry and clothing that span from prehistoric to contemporary times. This museum will please children of all ages. The museum is open Tuesday through Sunday, 10am to 5pm. It is closed on New Year's day, Easter Sunday, Thanksgiving and Christmas Day. Adult admission is $6 for NM residents, $9 nonresidents; youth 16 and under are free; students with id get a $1 discount.

ALL YEAR ROUND OUTDOOR ACTIVITIES

Samuel Perez Park

Also known as the "train park" because of the real locomotive located in the park. This park also features a multi-level play structure with slides, swings, and ramps. Free.

601 Alta Vista at St. Francis

Wilford Gallery Wind Sculpture Garden

Enjoy a hundred wind sculptures blowing in the breeze. 505-982-2403. Free.

403 Canyon Road

Black Canyon Trail

A short and easy one mile trail through an aspen and fir forest and located only 7 miles from the Plaza. In the summer lots of wildflowers and butterflies can be seen. In the winter, this is an easy trail to practice snow shoeing. The elevation is approximately 7,680 feet.

Drive about 7 miles on Hyde Park Road until you see the Black Canyon campground on the right. Parking is on the immediate left as you first enter and is free. You can also park in the campground for a $10 vehicle fee.

Camel Rock

Ten minutes outside of town is a great rock formation called Camel Rock. It is basically a very large rock that looks like a camel sitting down. There is a giant lower rock with a large rock on top. There is a parking lot and short, easy trail that leads to the rock. In looking at the rock from the other side, there is a strong resemblance to the movie character E.T. Rumor has it that Steven Spielberg photographed the face on the rock and used it as a basis for his main character in the movie.

Take US Highway 84/285 north to Exit 175. Drive to the west side service road and turn north and you will see the parking lot. The rock is directly across from the Camel Rock Casino.

Aspen Vista Hike

Throughout the year, this is the most popular trail in all of the Sangre de Christo Mountains. The trail starts out very gradual so it is very nice walking through the aspens, even with small children. Roundtrip the trail is 12 miles with a fairly large elevation change so make sure you only go a half mile or so from the parking lot before turning around. In the fall, the aspens turning colors are spectacular and this is one of the best places in New Mexico to see them. Snow starts falling on the trail in October and this is also an excellent trail for snowshoeing, which will be discussed in the Winter section of this book. The elevation at the start of this trail is approximately 9,000 feet.

Take Hyde Park Road for about 13 miles and the parking lot is on the right. There is a picnic area, bathrooms and ample parking. Free.

Trail at Tsankawe/Bandelier

Although about a half hour north of Santa Fe, this little known hike is a favorite among children because of the 4 wooden climbing ladders that are found along the trail and caves where Indians lived that can be explored. A civilization of approximately 1000 individuals lived on this breathtaking mesa in the 1400s and then left in the 1500s because of an extended drought. The trail is 1 ½ miles in length. The village ruins are reached after the trial winds through cliffs covered with petroglyphs (rock carvings) and climbs to the top of the mesa.

350 collapsed rooms and petroglyphs (rock carvings) can be seen along with many pieces of broken pottery. Be advised, however, that it is a federal offense to remove any broken pottery and the place is posted warning of the steep fines for those who violate this rule. As nice as this trail is, I have never seen more than a half a dozen people exploring it on any given day. It is **not** handicapped accessible. Young children 4 and older especially like climbing the wooden ladders.

Fees- This is a National Monument and fees of $12 per car must be left in the box. Or, a National Parks pass can be left on the windshield.

Take US highway 84/285 North to State Highway 502 West Los Alamos Exit. Turn left onto Los Alamos Highway to State Highway 4 West via the ramp to Bandelier National Monument/White Rock. Less than 1/4 of a mile past this turn Tsankawi will be located on the left hand side of the road. There are no signs for Tsankawi on Highway 4. If you get to the stoplight, you've gone too far. A large gravel parking area adjacent to the highway and a sign on the fence will indicate you've found the place.

Bandelier National Monument

Although about an hour drive from Santa Fe, this 33,000 acre canyon is beautiful and displays evidence of human presence going back over 11,000 years. There are guided and self-guided tours to learn about the ancient Pueblo Indians who lived here from about 1000 to the mid-1500s. There are numerous petroglyphs carved into rock walls, caves, ladders to climb and ruins. Note that this park can get crowded with tourists in the summer months and can be hot and dry in June with afternoon thunderstorms in July and August. It has a museum with films, a gift shop and restaurants.

Fees- This is a National Monument and fees of $12 per car are required or a National Parks pass.

15 Entrance Road, Los Alamos, NM 87544. 505-672-3861. Take US Highway 84/285 north to Take Saint Francis Drive (HWY 84/285) north toward Los Alamos. After passing Pojoaque, merge right onto New Mexico 502 to Los Alamos. Continue up 502 toward Los Alamos. Bear right and exit onto New Mexico 4 towards White Rock. Continue for 12 miles, passing White Rock. Bandelier's entrance is on your left.

Randall Davey Audubon Center & Sanctuary

Not far from the Plaza is this 135 acre peaceful sanctuary for plants, animals and visitors. From meadows to pine forests, this is an excellent park to enjoy nature. It is open Monday-Saturday from 8am-4pm. Free. Docent tour Fridays for $5, and Saturdays at 8am there are bird watching tours which are free.

1800 Upper Canyon Road. 505-983-4609.

Skateboard Park

Opened in 2011, this is considered to be the best skateboard park in Santa Fe. Free and fun.

302 W. DeVargas Street

Ghost Walks and Tours

Although not for small children, teenagers will like Santa Fe ghost walks. Most enjoyable in the summer, ghost walks and tours are available year round. For further information see Ghost Walks and Tours in the summer section.

Shidoni Foundry and Galleries

Five miles north of Santa Fe in the village of Tesuque is an eight acre sculpture garden to explore in a former apple orchid. There are also art galleries.

Free. Sculpture garden is open during daylight hours all year round. Bronze gallery Monday-Saturday 9am-5pm, Art Gallery Tuesday-Saturday 9am-5pm.

1508 Bishops Lodge Road, 505-988-8001.

Bike Riding

There are many places to ride bicycles in the Santa Fe area. Bike riding is great in the summer, spring and fall. There are a number of establishments that rent road bikes and mountain bikes in Santa Fe along with obtaining maps.

Mellow Velo, 132 East Marcy Street, 505-995-8356

New Mexico Bike & Sport, 524 C Cordova Drive, 505-820-0809

Santa Fe Mountain Sports, 1221 Flagman Way Suite B1, 505-988-3337

CHAPTER 2

WINTER IN SANTA FE

Crisp cold nights and bright sunny days are what you can expect in Santa Fe in the winter months. In addition to the year round activities listed above, there are many activities that can only be enjoyed in the winter. The average high and low temperatures in December are 43 and 18 degrees. In January they are 44 and 18 degrees and in February they are 48 and 22 degrees.

Christmas Eve on Canyon Road

One of Santa Fe's longest and nicest traditions is the holiday Canyon Road Farolito Walk in the evening on Christmas Eve. "Farolito" is Spanish for paper lantern and sand filled paper bags lit with candles inside line the historic neighborhood streets, art gallery gardens and adobe walls. Canyon Road, where most of the Santa Fe art galleries are located, is closed to traffic. People stop to sing in front of luminarias or small bon fires to celebrate the holidays. It is usually about 20 degrees at night, so dress warmly, and for some strange reason it usually snows on Christmas Eve. Children of all ages and babies wrapped warmly in strollers all enjoy the festivities. Many of the galleries are open this evening and offer free warm beverages to the visitors. This is a Santa Fe must for those who find themselves in Santa Fe over the Christmas holidays.

Free. Starts at dusk on Christmas Eve.

Sleigh Riding

Although there are many areas in the mountains just outside of Santa Fe for sleigh riding with small hills (Black Canyon listed above is one such place which usually has snow even when Hyde

Park Memorial State Park does not), the best place for sledding is Hyde Park Memorial State Park. This is the old and original ski area of the 1930s for Santa Fe and it is now a great sledding park. This park was New Mexico's first state park and is located in the Sangre de Christo Mountains not too far from Santa Fe's Plaza. Santa Fe has a Kmart and two Walmarts if you need to buy a sled.

A day pass is $5 per vehicle.

740 Hyde Park Road, about 10 minutes from town on the right.

Snowshoeing

Snowshoeing is a great way to enjoy the beautiful mountain areas just outside Santa Fe. Snowshoes can be bought at Sam's Club on Rodeo Road or REI in Santa Fe. If you would like to rent snow shoes, REI in the Railyard rents them (505-982-3557) as does Cottam's at Hyde Park, which is halfway up the ski mountain road. 505-982-0495.

Some of the best places to snowshoes include Black Canyon Trial and the Aspen Vista Trail listed above although many of the other trails nearby are also very good.

For those who prefer to have a guide to take them snowshoeing, Outspire of Santa Fe at 505-660-0394 does an excellent job of taking people with no experience, or with experience, on a 2 to 3 hour snowshoe adventure in the mountains about 30 minutes from the Santa Fe Plaza. They provide snowshoes, snow gaiters, sunscreen, daypack, bottled water and trail snacks along with a knowledgeable guide. They can also provide box lunches.

Skiing

When most people think of New Mexico they think of the desert and skiing never even crosses their mind. Ski Santa Fe, at 12,075 feet, however, is the second highest ski mountain in the Rockies, second only to Breckenridge which is 12,998 feet. The ski mountain has 7 lifts and 67 trails and 19 feet of snow on average each winter and with no crowds, Ski Santa Fe is a skiers paradise. And, it has great programs for kids.

Day Care 3 months to 3 years all day (8:30am-4:30pm) $90. Half day $70. Daycare by the hour $25. Children are separated by age and snacks and lunch are provided.

Snow Play all day is a fun introduction to the skiing environment with indoor and outdoor play with games and activities. Ages 3-4 (must be toilet trained) (8:30am-4:30pm). Half day (8:30am-1pm, and 12noon to 4:30pm) $75.

Lil' Chips Ski Program. Introduction to skiing for 3 & 4 year olds. Full day complete package (8:30am-4:30pm) includes a two hour lesson in the morning, lift ticket, rentals, helmet, lunch and snacks. The afternoon consists of snow play activities and games. All day package $127. Half day is a two hour lesson, lift ticket, rentals, helmet, lunch and snack. (8:30am-1:00pm or 12noon-to 4:30pm) $102. During holidays only full day packages are sold.

Chipmunk Ski Classes. Ages 6 & 7, 7-11. Kids are placed into classes according to their age and ability. Full day complete package (8:30am-4:30pm) includes a two hour lesson in the morning, lift ticket, rentals, helmet, lunch and snacks. The afternoon consists of snow play activities and games. All day package $127. Half day is a two hour lesson, lift ticket, rentals, helmet, lunch and snack. (8:30am-1:00pm or 12noon-to 4:30pm) $102. During holidays only full day packages are sold.

Snowboard packages. All day $135, half day $110. During holidays only full day packages are available.

The above rates are the current listed rates for the 2013/2014 ski season.

Reservations are required. Call 505-988-9636

In addition to Ski Santa Fe (505-982-4429), ski equipment can be rented at Cottam's at Hyde Park, which is halfway up the ski mountain road. 505-982-0495, Ski-Tech (505-983-5512 and Santa Fe Mountain Sports (505-988-3337).

CHAPTER 3

SPRING IN SANTA FE

Spring in Santa Fe is the least crowded season. April's average high temperature during the day reaches 65 degrees with a low of 32 at night, while May has an average temperature of 74 during the day and 41 at night. In April, the Farmers' Market, listed above in all year round activities, moves outside. This is a great time of year to hike and explore the Indian caves and petroglyphs. Flowers and trees begin blooming and the white water rafting season begins.

White Water Rafting

White water rafting in New Mexico can be very exciting as well as peaceful. A number of companies operate in Santa Fe and will take you on an approximate one hour drive for a trip on the Rio Grande or Rio Chama rivers. The season usually begins in April and lasts into the summer. Trips can last a half a day or full day and vary from class 1v thrilling rapids to calm river floats. Children 4 and up are usually welcome for the more calm trips and 7 and up for some of the other trips. Call for pricing and for reservations.

Kokopelli Rafting 505-983-3734, 800-879-9035

Santa Fe Rafting 505-988-4914, 888-988-4914

New Mexico River Adventurers 800-983-7756

Hiking and Exploring

As mentioned in the all year round activities, springtime in Santa Fe is a great time to hike and explore the Indian ruins and petroglyphs at Tsankawe and Bandelier National Monument as well as riding out to see Camel Rock. Note that if you hike in the area of the ski mountain, sometimes there is still snow on the ground right up until the beginning or middle of June and temperatures can be 15 degrees colder than at the Santa Fe Plaza.

CHAPTER 4

SUMMER IN SANTA FE

Summer in Santa Fe finds the most tourists since the season is long and temperate. Warm summer days and cool nights make for a perfect summer getaway for outdoor activities and dining, both inside and outside. And almost any evening will find a beautiful sunset over the Jemez Mountains. The average high and low in July is 86 and 55 degrees, and in August it is 83 and 53 degrees.

Santa Fe Bandstand

From approximately the third week in June to the third week in August the Santa Fe Plaza has free outdoor concerts at 6pm and 7:15pm. Locals bring blankets and lawn chairs and picnics to enjoy this free outdoor experience.

Music on the Hill, Saint John's College

This popular summer event is in its ninth season and takes place in June and July at 1160 Camino Cruz Blanca. 505-984-600. Once again locals bring blankets and lawn chairs and picnics to enjoy music in this mountain setting. Free concert dates already scheduled for 2014 are June 11, 18 and 25 and July 9, 16 and 23.

Santa Fe Rodeo

The Rodeo de Santa Fe has been going on for the last 64 years and usually takes place the third week of June. It is considered to be one of the top 60 rodeos in the country, draws over 500 contestants and usually includes world champion cowboys. Each of the performances includes all the competitive events – individual and team roping, steer wrestling, barrel racing, saddle and bareback bronco riding and bull riding. There are many things to do for kids. The Mutton Bustin' (for children over 4 and under 60 pounds) and youth barrel racers continue to be a crowd favorite. There is also a carnival midway, concessions, vendors and a beer garden.

Tickets are $10 for children 10 and under and adults 65 and over are also $10. Other ticket prices are $17, $22, or $27.

Rodeo de Santa Fe is located at 3237 Rodeo Road, about 15 or 20 minutes from downtown Santa Fe. There are two entrances to the Rodeo coming from Rodeo Road; one off Richards Avenue and the other off Paseo de los Pueblos.

El Rancho de las Golondrinas

El Rancho de Las Golondrinas ("Ranch of the Swallows") is a living history museum and is located about a half an hour or twenty minute drive south of Santa Fe's Plaza. This historic ranch dates back to the early 1700s and was an important stopping point before wagons reached Santa Fe along the famous Camino Real from Mexico City. It is located in a rural farming community and it shows life in early New Mexico. The museum is open for self-guided tours from June through September, Wednesday-Sunday, 10am to 4pm. Adults are $6, teens $4 and children under 12 are free.

There are also many great weekend events in the summer at El Rancho de Las Golondrinas including a Children's Fair, an Herb and Lavender Fair, a Fiber Arts Festival, the Viva Mexico Celebration, a Summer Festival, Children's Celebration Festival, and a Renaissance Fair. Typical fees for the events are adults $8, teens and seniors $5, and children 12 and under free.

334 Los Pinos Road, Santa Fe. Take Exit 276 off I-25 and follow the Las Golondrinas signs. 505-471-2261

White Water Rafting

White water rafting in New Mexico can be very exciting as well as peaceful. A number of companies operate in Santa Fe and will take you on an approximate one hour drive for a trip on the Rio Grande or Rio Chama rivers. The season usually begins in April and lasts into the summer. Trips can last a half a day or full day and vary from class 1v thrilling rapids to calm river floats. Children 4 and up are usually welcome for the more calm trips and 7 and up for some of the other trips. Call for pricing, age restrictions and for reservations.

Kokopelli Rafting 505-983-3734, 800-879-9035

Santa Fe Rafting 505-988-4914, 888-988-4914

New Mexico River Adventurers 800-983-7756

Zozobra

The burning of Zozobra, or Old Man Gloom, is an 88 year old tradition that takes place the first Thursday in September of each year. Zozobra is a giant wooden and cloth marionette that waves and growls when it is burned. It is stuffed with thousands of shredded papers, which traditionally includes old police reports, paid-off mortgages, divorce papers, and tales of woe and bad luck and sorrows for the year just past submitted by people of all ages. It is the hope of all of the individuals who submit these papers that they will disappear into the smoke and flames of the burned puppet. Food and drink are provided by numerous vendors and music fills the air. Fireworks go off overhead while the crowd cheers.

At dark at Fort Marcy Park, a short walk from the Plaza. There is a fee to enter the park. Tickets for the event were $10 in 2013 with children under 10 free.

Viewing Prairie Dogs

Children of all ages are fascinated by prairie dogs. Although they can sometimes be spotted in fields in Santa Fe, there are two spots where they can be seen in the summer. One is the shops at Jackalope on Cerrillios Road which has a prairie dog village. The other is in Frenchy's Park, where they can be viewed and photographed in the wild. Frenchy's Park is 17 acres and also has a playground.

Frenchy's Park, Aqua Fria and Osage Street

Jackalope, 2820 Cerrillos Road, (505)471-8539

Ghost Walks and Tours

Although not for young children, teenagers and adults will enjoy Santa Fe ghost walks which take place in the historic downtown Plaza area in the evenings.

Allan's Tours 505-986-5002 or 505-231-1336

Original Santa Fe Ghost Tour, Peter or Liz 505-983-7774

Bike Riding

There are a number of establishments that rent road bikes and mountain bikes in Santa Fe along with obtaining maps.

Mellow Velo, 132 East Marcy Street, 505-995-8356

New Mexico Bike & Sport, 524 C Cordova Drive, 505-820-0809

Santa Fe Mountain Sports, 1221 Flagman Way Suite B1, 505-988-3337

CHAPTER 5

FALL IN SANTA FE

Many locals will confide that fall in Santa Fe is their favorite season. September finds highs of 78 degrees and lows of 48. October finds highs of 67 and lows of 36. With the smells of pinion wood burning in fireplaces, the end of September to the middle of October finds the aspen trees in golden colors. Fall is the perfect time for walking, hiking and bike riding. It also fairly common to have snowfalls in the mountains in October. One October 8th we rode the chairlift one way up to the top of the ski mountain and then walked down in about 8 inches of snow.

The Turning Colors of Aspen Leaves

Probably the best place to view the changing aspen colors in the fall is the ride in your car up Hyde Park Road to the top of the mountains which end at Ski Santa Fe. There are many places along the road to pull over and admire the view and to take photos. The most spectacular views are probably at Aspen Vista. Some of the areas have picnic tables. The leaves usually start changing around the beginning of October and last a few weeks. It is also not unusual to see snow at this time of year.

Chairlift at Ski Santa Fe

View the beautiful changing colors of the aspen trees on the fall scenic chair lift at Ski Santa Fe. Usually runs weekends from the beginning of September to the middle of October each fall. 10am to 3pm. 1 way $8 (walk back down), roundtrip $12, and under 46" and over 72 years of age free. Bring a jacket, and maybe a hat and gloves, since it is usually 15 to 20 degrees colder than the temperature at the Plaza

Take Hyde Park Road until it ends, about a half an hour ride from the Plaza.

Albuquerque International Balloon Fiesta

A world renowned and the largest balloon event in the world for children of all ages in this 78 acre park. You can get up close to the balloons as they are inflated or take balloon rides. There is a morning session at dawn and an evening session at dusk. It is suggested that you arrive at 4:30-5am for the morning session and at 4pm for the evening events. There are over 550 balloons including 100 special shape balloons. Numerous vendors sell souvenirs and food and there is also daily entertainment. This is a must see event if you are in Santa Fe the first week of October and it takes about 45 minutes to an hour to drive to the park from Santa Fe.

October 4-12, 2014, October 3-11, 2015 and October 1-9, 2016. Kids 12 and under free, others $8 per person.

Take I25 South for about 45 minutes to Balloon Fiesta Park, 4401 Alameda NE, Albuquerque. 505-821-1000.

Bike Riding

There are a number of establishments that rent road bikes and mountain bikes in Santa Fe along with obtaining maps.

Mellow Velo, 132 East Marcy Street, 505-995-8356

New Mexico Bike & Sport, 524 C Cordova Drive, 505-820-0809

Santa Fe Mountain Sports, 1221 Flagman Way Suite B1, 505-988-3337

Chapter 6

SANTA FE KID FRIENDLY RESTAURANTS

As mentioned in the introduction, Santa Fe has 429 restaurants. This includes the usual fast food restaurants such as McDonald's, Wendy's, Burger King, Dairy Queen, Subway, Carl's Jr., Panda Express, Arby's, Taco Bell, KFC, Sonic, Long John Silver, Domino's, Pizza Hut, Church's Chicken, and Quiznos, as well as chains such as Outback, Chili's, the Olive Garden, Panera, Wings, Baskin Robbins, Red Lobster, Applebee's, among others. Since you can eat at these fast food and restaurant chains at home, the following 20 kid friendly restaurants do not include fast food nor restaurant chains.

The Shed

New Mexican, just off the Plaza, 113 E. Palace Ave., 505-982-9030

11am-2:30pm, 5:30pm-9pm seven days a week

Tia Sophia

New Mexican, just off the Plaza, 210 W. San Francisco St., 505-983-9880

Kid's menu

Mon.-Sat. 7am-2pm, Sun. 8am-1pm

Burrito Company

New Mexican, just off the Plaza, 111 Washington Ave., 505-982-4453

Kid's menu

Mon.-Fri. 7:30am-5pm, Sun. 8am-5pm

Cowgirl BBQ

Barbeque & sandwiches & more, 319 S. Guadalupe St., 505-982-2565

Kid's menu

Mon.-Fri. 11:30am-10:30pm, Sat.-Sun. 11am-11pm

Upper Crust Pizza

Pizza & sandwiches, just off the Plaza, 329 Old Santa Fe Trail, 505-982-0000

11am-11pm daily

Maria's

New Mexican, 555 W. Cordova Road, 505-983-7929

Kid's menu 12 and under

Mon.-Fri. 11am-10pm, Sat.-Sun. noon-10pm

Harry's Roadhouse

Comfort food & New Mexican, 96 Old Las Vegas Highway, 505-989-4629

Kid's menu

7am-9:30pm every day

Hagan Dazs Shop

Ice cream, on the Plaza, 56 E. San Francisco Street, 505-988-3858

Ellie's Yoberri Park

Frozen yogurt, 326 W. San Francisco, 505-995-1191

Sun.-Thur. 12:30pm-8:00pm, Fri.-Sat. 12:30pm-9pm

Flying Tortilla

New Mexican, 4250 Cerrillos Rd., 505-424-1680

6:30am-9pm every day

Pantry Restaurant

American & Mexican, 1820 Cerrillos Rd., 505-986-0022

Mon.-Sat. 6:30am-8:30pm, Sun. 7am-8:30pm

Tune Up Café

Continental & New Mexican, 1115 Hickox, 505-983-7060

Mon.-Fri. 7am-10pm, Sat.-Sun. 8am-10pm

Yummy Café

Asian, 1616 St. Michaels Drive, 505-466-1681

Mon.-Thur. 11am-9pm, Fri. 11am-9:30pm, Sat. 4pm-9:30pm, Sun. 4pm-9pm

Los Potrillos Family Mexican Restaurant & Bar

Mexican, 1947 Cerrillos Rd., 505-992-0550

Sun.-Mon. 11am-10pm, Tue.-Wed. 11am-11pm, Thur. 11am-11:30pm, Fri.-Sat. 11am-12am

Mucho Gusto

Mexican, 839 Paseo de Peralta St., 505-955-8402

Mon.-Sat. 11am-9pm

La Choza

Mexican, 905 Alarid St., 505-982-0909

Kid's menu

Mon.-Sat. 11am-2:30pm, 5pm-9pm

Zia Diner

Comfort food, 326 S. Guadalupe St., 505-988-7008

Open daily 7am-close at night

Tomasita's

New Mexican, 505 S. Guadalupe St., 505-983-5721

Kid's menu for children under 10

Mon.-Thur. 11am-9pm, Sat.-Sun. 11am-10pm

Flying Star Café

American, in Railyard at 500 Market Street, 505-216-3939

Sun.-Thur. 7am-9pm, Fri.-Sat. 7am-10pm

Bumble Bee's Baja Grill

Mexican, 301 Jefferson Street (505-820-2862) and 3777 Cerrillos (505-988-3278)

Kid's menu 10 and under

11am-9pm daily

Other Books by the Author

I hope you enjoyed this book on Santa Fe New Mexico with Kids. If it helps you to more fully enjoy the great city of Santa Fe I have accomplished my purpose.

If you enjoyed this book, I would really appreciate it if you could take a few moments and share your thoughts by posting a review on Amazon.

Feel free to also take a look at the other book that I have authored on Amazon. The title is "Get Rid Of Your Debt And Avoid Bankruptcy" and can be found at the following link.

http://www.amazon.com/Your-Debt-Avoid-Bankruptcy-ebook/dp/B00FQSNTIQ

Made in the USA
Coppell, TX
28 March 2022